"This groundbreaking set of beautiful little books doesn't fit a mold and is wonderfully suitable for all audiences. The best part about *Suicide Survivors' Club* is that they were written ten years after the family's horrific loss. While every survivor of suicide has a book to write, a story to tell, it's often written too soon and without the hope and healing that comes from time. *Suicide Survivors' Club* will become a go-to when I recommend books for survivors."

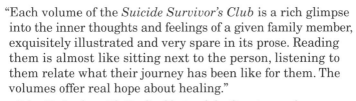

– *American Association of Suicidology*

"Each volume of the *Suicide Survivor's Club* is a rich glimpse into the inner thoughts and feelings of a given family member, exquisitely illustrated and very spare in its prose. Reading them is almost like sitting next to the person, listening to them relate what their journey has been like for them. The volumes offer real hope about healing."

– John R. Jordan, *Ph.D., Co-Chair of the Survivors of Suicide Loss Task Force of the National Action Alliance for Suicide Prevention*

"This beautifully illustrated 5-book set depicts the aftermath of a husband/father's suicide through the eyes and in the words of his wife and children. The brief books explore the feelings of suicide loss survivors of any age and the healing power of art. The fifth book, *Parenting the Suicide Survivors' Club*, is a short memoir by mom Rebecca that reflects the challenges of holding a family together as the sole remaining parent."

– *American Foundation f___ _____ _____*

D0897116

Suicide Survivors' Club: Becky is a Story Portrait™ using narrative fragments excerpted from interviews with Becky. The pieces of the story are arranged to graph her shifting emotions, from high/ecstatic (Heaven) to low/desperate (Hell). For more information on the artistic process, please see page 42.

Second edition printed 2019 in USA
ISBN 978-0-9971454-0-3

Order books at SuicideSurvivorsClub.org or Amazon.com

Published by SSC Publishing

Helpful Resources

If you or someone else is at immediate risk of suicide, call 911
National Suicide Prevention Lifeline: 1-800-273-TALK (8255)
Crisis Text Line: text 741741
Trevor Project (LGBTQ): 1-866-488-7386 / thetrevorproject.org
Trans Lifeline: hotline 877-565-8860 / translifeline.org
American Foundation for Suicide Prevention: afsp.org
National Alliance on Mental Illness (NAMI): nami.org
NAMI Minnesota: 1-888-NAMI-HELPS (626-4435) / namimn.org

Suicide Survivors' Club

A Family's Journey Through the Death of Their Loved One

Becky

by Laurie Phillips

Foreword

"Look at what these people did with their own hands," I first thought when I saw the *Suicide Survivors' Club* books. Beyond their usefulness to anyone who has been affected by the suicide of a person close to them, there is also a benefit to the larger realm of individuals who are touched by the experiences of survivors of suicide. That group includes nearly everyone in the helping professions, as well as anyone who knows a family that has lost a member by suicide.

Central to my understanding of grieving is the healing power of doing something with your eyes, hands, and body — anything that creates a product, a result, a process — that supports the interplay between the head, the heart, and the body. The Andersons certainly have done a magnificent job of that in their lives over the decade after the suicide of their father and husband with the help of numerous people, including the artist Laurie Phillips.

Their process is vast, ranging from adoration of his uniqueness and complexity to resentment for what he did to them, neither over-idealizing nor blaming. This is not a neat package of suggestions or guidelines; rather it gives permission to stay with the incomprehensibility of it all, to seek closure but know that it will never come completely, to tolerate the ambiguity of the *why* questions and the meaning of their own surprising reactions in daily life. It's impressive how many people have been involved in this family's healing, some deliberately invited in, and others included by the normal contact of everyday living. The family manages to allow for the event of the suicide and what follows to stay with them for as long as it takes until it no longer holds them in its grip.

These books should help readers to better comprehend the complexity of the process of recovery from the suicide of a loved one. It can't be sorted into neat boxes; it takes a long long long time, and much of it involves living an ordinary life, an ordinary life that makes acres of room for grieving and healing. The artwork beautifully augments the words in the books, making for a fuller understanding and bigger impact of the narratives. The books are deeply moving, informational, and give permission to trust in finding one's own way through such a horrific loss.

David Morris, *Ph.D.*
Licensed Psychologist

heaven

Don and I set specific goals
for our marriage. We've had
a good summer in spite of
all the problems.

Don spirals out of control. There
are hurtful exchanges. I insist
on us sleeping in separate rooms.

hell

He is irrational, impossible to deal with. I've seen him this way before. I hear him rummaging around in the basement. I'm afraid. I call his therapist.

Don takes the kids to school. I call several times to ask him to meet me for lunch so we can talk. He refuses. I know something is wrong.

He doesn't show up to meet me and the kids for their swimming lesson. I call Pattie and ask if he called her. She says no. I don't want to call 911 so I ask a family friend to see if her father, the local fire chief, can send a police car to the park where I believe Don is.

Two squad cars pull up and come to the door and ask my name. They tell me Don has killed himself.

I call Pattie and tell her to come home.

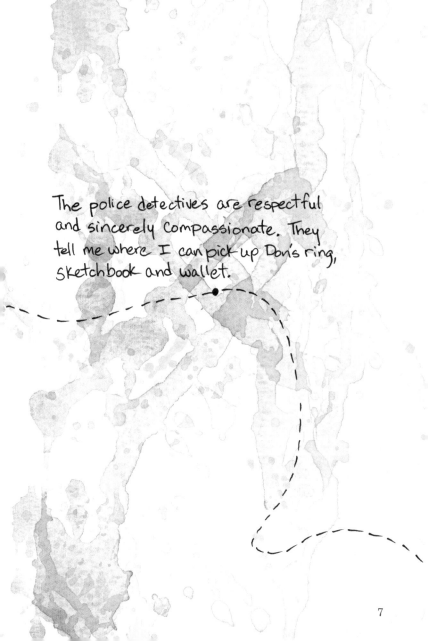

The police detectives are respectful and sincerely compassionate. They tell me where I can pick up Don's ring, sketchbook and wallet.

7

I tell Pattie
what happened.

I'm overwrought with anxiety about the legal and financial implications and how it will affect the three kids.

9

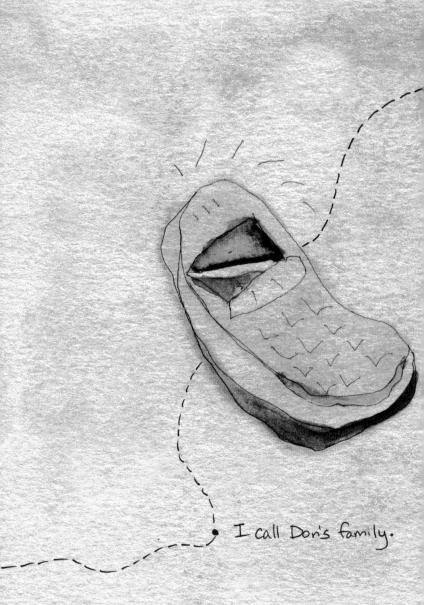

I call Don's family.

I get calls from detectives,
the coroner's office, our minister, the
kid's teachers, staff and social workers.

People bring food
and flowers.
They write, call
and come over.
The outpouring
of love is
phenomenal.

A woman from the
coroner's office calls
to say she'll be riding
with Don's body to
the funeral home.
She tells me he
will not be alone.
She comments on
how beautiful his
hands are. I'm
deeply touched by
her sensitivity.

I go to the funeral home with Don's sister and a friend. Don is wrapped in a sheet. His beautiful hands are on his chest. I can feel his presence in the viewing room. I don't want to stay and I don't want to leave. I stay and talk to him.

Pattie refuses
to see her father's
body. We leave
letters with him.

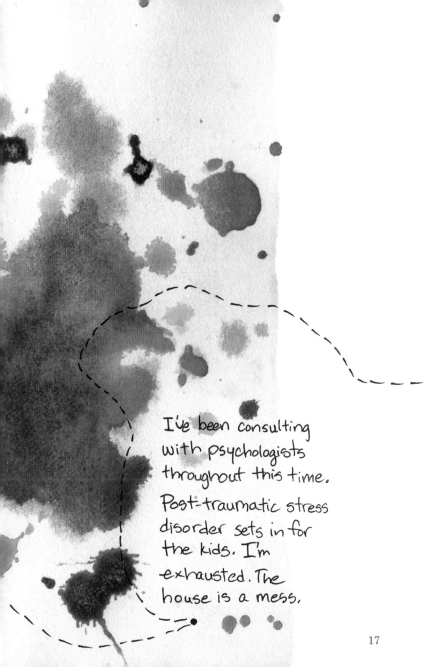

I've been consulting
with psychologists
throughout this time.
Post-traumatic stress
disorder sets in for
the kids. I'm
exhausted. The
house is a mess.

17

Pattie goes back to college. We fight a lot even though we need each other desperately.

We celebrate Halloween, Thanksgiving and Christmas. It's bleak and painful.

The legal paperwork
is endless: banks,
lawyers, social security,
taxes, wills.

I start culling through Don's possessions. I keep shutting down. My brother-in-law comes from out of town to help me organize. He spends a lot of time talking with me.

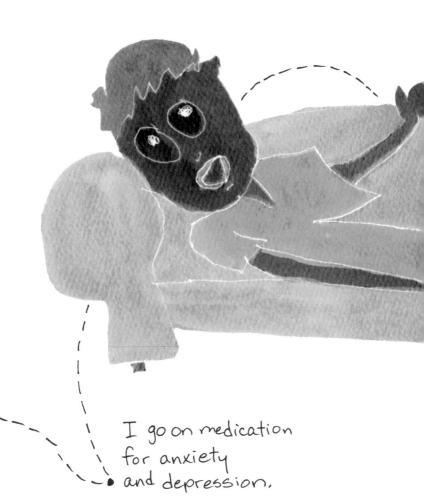

I go on medication
for anxiety
and depression.

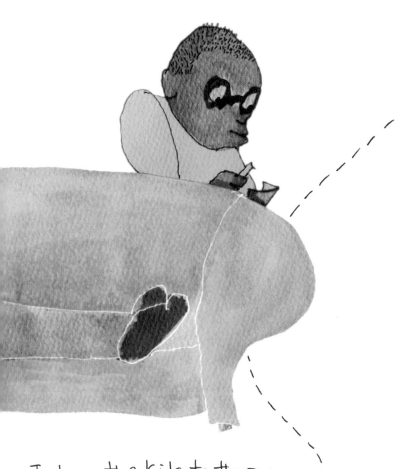

I drive the kids to therapy twice a week. They're having a very hard time. It's so intense.

My older son
helps me decide
not to sell
the house.
We plant lots
of flowers
instead.

We're all doing
the best we can.
It's a blur.

One year later we have a funeral service to bury some of Don's ashes in a beautiful Catholic cemetery. Before I purchase the plot a wonderful woman who works at the church gives me a "tour" of all the people who are buried near Don. She tells me about who they were. Don's new next-door neighbor loved to play cards.

The police make
extra patrols
by our house.
People are
overwhelmingly
kind and thoughtful.
Except the two
workmen who were
fired because
they were stealing
from us.

The second year is horrible.

29

The kids and I are very open about the suicide.

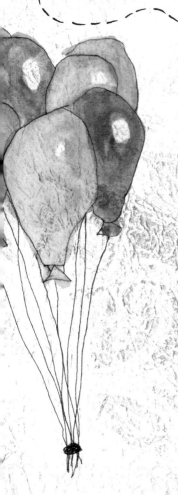

I organize a fundraiser for a suicide prevention group (SAVE). It's a large undertaking and very rewarding.

31

I try to find books for children on suicide. I can't find any that handle the material in a way I believe would help the kids. I'm encouraged to consider writing one.

I scatter the rest of Don's ashes in the lake. Things are better, but they're not. I feel as though I'll never recover. Sadness settles in.

I start dating again.
Not good. Practice
makes it better.
I have a few
good dates.

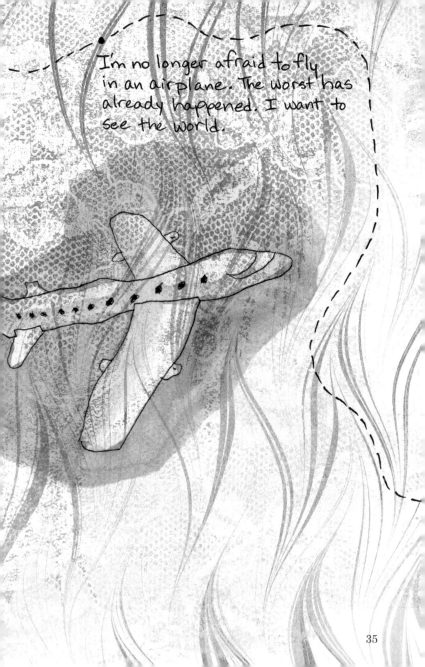

I'm no longer afraid to fly in an airplane. The worst has already happened. I want to see the world.

After three years I'm still
getting rid of Don's clutter.
I resent it at times and
feel very sad at other times.

Four years later, all three
kids are active and happy.
We've been altered as a family.
Nothing can take away the close
bond we share.

Ten years later: I couldn't have imagined the thriving people we've become. We never forget the shattering loss but we all feel proud of the full lives we've created.
heaven
hell

Epilogue

"Life is filled with change. I'm in the midst of preparing my boys Aidan and Will for college and find myself fluctuating between emotions of great joy and tears from missing them. I made the big decision to leave our home of 26 years; packing up keepsakes for Pattie and the boys now. I feel gratified that I have created a multifaceted life and experienced love again. Looking forward… I see a vital future."

Rebecca Anderson

Acknowledgements

Thank you to the many people who helped make the Suicide Survivors' Club books a reality: Meg Anderson for her philanthropic support and for her belief in our mission, Burt Nordstrand Family Foundation, and generous donors to our Indiegogo campaign and Book Drive.

Thank you to mental health professionals Henry Emmons, MD, John R. Jordan, Ph.D., Noel Larson, Ph.D., Sue Towey, RN, CNS, MS, LP, Janice Winchester Nadeau, Ph.D., LP, RN, David Morris, Ph.D., and Sharon Ward, MA, LPC, LP, for their endorsements and support.

Thank you to NAMI Minnesota for promoting mental health and suicide prevention, partnering with us, and distributing the books to suicide loss survivors.

Thank you to our communications expert and strategic advisor Louise Woehrle. We value her guidance in publishing the books, editorial contributions, and leadership in developing opportunities to help grow SSC in ways that support suicide loss survivors.

Special thanks to the Anderson children, Pattie, Aidan, and Will who shared their stories so people would know there is a way to rebuild your life after such a tragic event.

Art Transforms Trauma

It's been a soulful experience to work with Rebecca Anderson and her three children on the *Suicide Survivors' Club* book series. I feel honored to have been entrusted with their stories and have tried my best to represent their intimate experiences.

The vision Rebecca and I share for this project is to reduce the stigma of suicide and make a difficult subject easier to discuss with family, friends, and communities. We believe storytelling can help transform senseless, overwhelming suffering and connect it to universal human experience.

The handwritten text in each of the four books — *Becky*, *Pattie*, *Aidan*, and *Will* — were taken from interviews with each family member. Then, I asked them to give me a number from plus 100 (the best they've ever felt) to minus 100 (the worst they've ever felt) for each text bit. That provided the plot points for the Heaven/Hell graph. Dashed lines connect all the story elements.

I've told the Andersons' stories through common illustrations they helped me choose. I used my less-dominant hand to re-draw and interpret the images to look raw and unpolished.

To learn more about my art process, please visit *www.suicidesurvivorsclub.org*.

Laurie Phillips

Authors

LAURIE PHILLIPS, artist, healer, author, speaker, and co-founder of SSC, LLC has worked as a public artist since 1992. She's served as a stress relief coach in hospitals and other organizations and is the co-founder of Museum Sage, an experience that combines life coaching and art appreciation. Laurie and Rebecca have co-presented on using art and narrative to heal from a traumatic experience at Mayo Clinic, NAMI Minnesota, American Association of Suicidology, Macalester College, and Children's Hospital.

REBECCA ANDERSON, LPN, LCSW, mother, medical professional, educator, and speaker, with a BS in Public Health/Sociology, is the author of *Parenting the Suicide Survivors' Club* and co-founder of SSC, LLC. She's worked as a nurse in maternal/child healthcare and as a medical social worker. Rebecca lost her husband to suicide in 2002. Eight years later she and her children embarked on a healing art/narrative journey with artist Laurie Phillips that resulted in the *Suicide Survivors' Club* 5-book set. She co-presents *Trauma Transformed Through Art and Narrative*.

Books from SSC Publishing

Suicide Survivors' Club is a family's personal journey through the suicide of husband and father Don, as told by wife and mother Rebecca and their three children, Pattie, Aidan, and Will. Each surviving family member's unique experience is documented in their own words within four individual books. Created by compassionate artist Laurie Phillips, the books tell their stories with moving words, short sentences, and poignant art graphed onto the pages — revealing the family's emotional ups and downs during the healing process. The fifth book, *Parenting the Suicide Survivors' Club,* a memoir written by Rebecca Anderson, completes the set and offers the perspective of a mother, wife, and medical professional determined to put her broken family back together again.

....

Healing After a Suicide Loss: All Ages Workbook & Activity Guide for families, friends, therapists, and facilitators is a companion guide to the *Suicide Survivors' Club* book set. It provides helpful questions and activities for survivors as they navigate grief and loss. A sample from the workbook can be found in *Will*, pages 18-19.

....

Please visit *www.suicidesurvivorsclub.org* for information about ordering books.